Going
On

Also by the author:

The Singing Road

Shining Star

Going On

by Nora Beth Main

The Naylor Company
Book Publishers of the Southwest
San Antonio, Texas

Library of Congress Cataloging in Publication Data

Main, Nora Elizabeth, 1885-
Going on.

Poems.
I. Title.
PS3525.A4154G6 811'.5'4 75-14151
ISBN 0-8111-0580-6

Printed in the United States of America

Dedicated
to those who can look back
with hope and glory . . . and
forward to the culmination
of both

Contents

Crossroads of Time

Going On

We come to crossroads in the valley haze
And hesitate in contemplative mood . . .
Sometimes we lengthen out the hours to days,
Or years . . . remaining there tho life seems crude.
We settle down to this environment,
Grow old, put out the candle once so bright . . .
The dream is over, we may sit content
With less of vision in this dreary plight.

But at the crossroads should you choose a road
And find the journey to be lesser fare,
That were far better than the squat abode
Of lost initiative and bleak despair.
Life has a dream . . . keep it forever new!
Keep going on, and make the dream come true!

Crossroads of Time

America, you have been true and brave,
With never a desire to desecrate
Or break a nation's spirit, to enslave
And exploit, leaving mortals desolate.
You are not perfect, nor submerged in sin;
Nor have you ever failed to teach the way
Of perfect principle and discipline . . .
Remembering, God brought you to this day.

The crucial hour of all your years is come,
The world is at the crossroads of all time;
One road permits no moratorium,
The other is immortal and sublime.
Choose now America . . . choose cautiously,
God stands beside the road to victory!

The Guiding Star

What would you have, O trav'ler of the night,
With heart so weary worn, and restless feet . . .
Is not the living water just in sight?
Along its banks green willows nod, and wheat
Is waving in the field beside the stream.
Lift once again your courage . . . for today
My friend, if you will look, a guiding beam
Will set your footsteps straight upon the way!

What would you have, O trav'ler of the night,
Except that faith reborn itself . . . that hope
Refresh your spirit with a radiant light.
Lift higher yet your head . . . Above the slope
'Tis bright . . . and brighter still for weary eyes,
To see the Star, that shines from Heaven's skies!

Double Decade

In retrospect, the thrilling twenty years
This pen has conjured sonnets for the press,
Implies a labor loved . . . altho some fears
That faulty technique might delay success.
But when I listened as they filled the air
From powerful stations in the South, I cried
In thankfulness, for friends who loved to share
My thoughts with others, sometimes nationwide.

From School and Church and University
Came honors, bearing high encouragement . . .
Whose gracious gifts were benedictory
And bowed my head in humble heart's content.
The double ten seems but a flash of light . . .
A world without a shadow or a night!

Lyndon to Lady Bird

We'll walk the way together, Lady Bird,
With one tall flaming goal to keep in mind –
We'll keep the faith, and trusting in His Word
Give ultimate in service to mankind.
We'll feel the sting of arrows piercing flesh
At unfamiliar crossroads we must face –
But He shall know, and prompt us and refresh
Our spirits by His gentle strength and grace.

The goal is luminous and seems quite near
As we begin to climb the upper trail;
The Lamp that never dims is high and clear
To guide our feet when storms of life assail.
It is for us who love the way He planned –
To guard, and cherish, this beloved Land!

Capacity for Greatness

So much is taken lightly as we live
And work among the hurried populace . . .
So little warmth and color do we give
Which might flash beauty on a tired face.
So small a note of praise is offered one
Whose silent genius is the only song
That stirs the pulses when a task is done . . .
When quite forgotten as the day grows long.

Ah, well, fame is not popularity!
Fame is the incense from a glowing mind
Left burning in the wake of one set free . . .
Genius surviving self, to bless mankind.
In smothered praise man feels his heart retire
As though God stood and breathed upon that fire!

White Roses

I'm sending you a rose as white as white,
And may you let it live within your heart
Secure and safe from tragic withered plight . . .
That it may keep its fresh unblemished start.
On earthly trails we mortals love to trod,
White roses live and grow along with us . . .
They spring from earth, in whiteness born of God,
That we may see His touch . . . how glorious!

There is a magic sensitivity
In whiteness pure as freshly falling snow . . .
In bridal gown so smooth and satiny,
Or touch of baby garments mothers know.
And in that Land where whiteness never dies
We'll read the answer in our Master's eyes!

The Poignant Cry

God of the universe look on thine own,
Look now, on suffering humanity
Upon a cross made by their hands alone . . .
Draw out the nails and let their hands fall free.
Do not forsake them in this bitter fare,
Hide not thy face from earth's bewildered throng;
True, once in ignorance, mankind could stare
At rugged beams and sing a rabble song.

Abide a little while, and they shall hear,
They shall repent and wash their hearts in blood
Still warm and dripping, where a piercing spear
Released a living, flowing, holy flood.
God . . . listen to the strange linguistic cry
As truth dawns on a world that should not die!

The Ceaseless Call

If you desire it, you may hear the call . . .
Sometimes it breaks against my troubled heart
Like echoes bounding from a waterfall,
Surprising life into a fresh new start.
The force of it always awakens me,
And listening, I hear His kindly voice . . .
Then I no longer sense futility;
The bright light of His glory floods my choice.

No longer shall this morbid consciousness
Enshroud itself in clouds of mortal gloom –
For light breaks thru, and quickly I profess
The Lord's omnipotence, and give Him room.
Then sudden glory lights a lost World's face,
His glory, shining thru redeeming grace!

Ancestors

They sought contentment in the Yesterday
With rumbling vehicles and oxen drawn . . .
With sunrise sending beams in reveille
To rouse the cabin and announce the dawn.
Where wildness fades into a distant blur
And weeks go by without a sign of life . . .
The same small stirrings, same vernacular,
In evidence that loneliness is rife.

Where panthers claw the cabin door at night
And barnyard ravishings betray the plot . . .
When illness came and death besought the cot,
They send a prayer to God to heal their plight.
Content to bear the hardship and the pain . . .
They labor ceaselessly to ease the strain!

Lest We Perish

The tangled meadow grasses, sere and dead,
Were once the emeralds of yesterday . . .
If we look back we'll miss the joys ahead
For peace and promise revel in their sway.
We hear the cry of peoples trapped in mire,
And having heard, it cannot be denied;
Altho not very wise, yet with desire
We counsel wisdom for the winning side.

God's empty children yearn for gracious fill
While hungry earth laps blood and cradles pain;
Encroaching evil leaves a mortal stain . . .
The treadmill of the world is dripping, still.
Not for a moment dare we look behind . . .
Nor veil our vision as if eyes were blind!

Nativity

His voice was deeply tender, as he said,
"We come from Nazareth, it must be here
We shall find shelter for the night . . . a bed,
Where she may rest and sleep and have no fear."
He looked upon the lovely one. "No room!"
The answer came . . . the restless noisy throng
Gave evidence as in the evening gloom
They go, but in their hearts they keep a song.

It could have been the faintest echoing
Of Heaven's a capella, far from earth . . .
So soon to burst the sky with caroling
The very moment of the Christ Child's birth.
They sought a lowly place to rest that night,
But Heaven found them with a star's bright light!

At Nazareth

The silent hills rise up protectingly
Above the endless arguing and fear . . .
The bleak dismay as none dared cry their plea,
Just hope Messiah's time was drawing near.
The whip of state stung like an adder's fang,
To poison faith and still their cherished dream . . .
For holy prophets wrote and Judah sang
Of a Deliverer to reign supreme.

Then of a sudden Nazareth awoke
And certain ones moved out along the road,
For Caesar's strict decree became a yoke . . .
A penalizing tax to bind and goad.
But one upon that journey was with child,
And riding a small beast she mused and smiled.

Only Believe

So many are amazed at the belief
In Christmas as the birthday of a King . . .
And doubt His power to assuage man's grief
Or heal the broken heart of suffering.
They look at tinsel and the weak disguise,
At poverty and wanton sin, the den . . .
And wonder if our faith is mere surmise,
That once He trod the earth as other men.

But on the holy hour when Jesus came
Judean hills were set ablaze with light,
And Angel choirs proclaimed the glorious name
Of Christ the Lord and Saviour, born that night.
And shall the living world believe and live,
Or judgment day still find it fugitive!

A Christmas Wish

I wish for you, a beautiful white snow,
A spread of dazzling crystal in the sun . . .
Trees glittering in jewels just for show
While jolly jingling sleigh bells join the fun.
May warm clad carolers sing thru the night,
And joyful shepherds riding on a sled
Leave Magi gifts beside each tiny bed . . .
While by one brilliant star, the world is bright.

May anxious hearts know comfort of the blest
As loved ones traveling, reach home in time,
And while the lonely welcome Him as guest
May bells of Heaven ring their sweetest chime.
And may the angel chorus sing again
The glory of God's peace, goodwill to men!

Christmas Bells

Upon the far horizon Christmas bells
Ring gaily as the morning light appears;
Around the world their soft sweet chiming tells
A story that should silence all our fears . . .
Above the sky-plane shines a star at night,
Above the battle strife a song is heard;
Beyond the black of hate is love's pure light,
Beyond the dying . . . life anew is stirred!

The patient Christmas bells ring out again,
Reminding of the gentle Saviour's birth;
Reminding – of goodwill and peace to men,
Of righteousness to cover all the earth.
Ring out gay carillons, until that day
When every evil thing shall fade away!

A Burst of Genius

Top officers profuse in praise – eyes wet,
Their voices harsh with bitterness to hide
The choking grief – that lads so young had met
And stopped the angry blast of surging tide.
The inborn saneness of humanity
Is slow to reconcile that wild outburst,
That fierce creative current leaping free . . .
Ere civilized restraint had quenched its thirst.

The latent wells of genius spring awake,
And streams of overwhelming virtue rise
To flood the timid soul of youth, and break
Upon the primitive in strange disguise.
This rush of genius is the war's death knell . . .
If it bring peace . . . the years alone will tell!

The Way

There is no peace a mortal may possess
Until the principles of truth ordain . . .
No freedom until love is free to reign,
For love and truth are born of righteousness.
Truth is the living spirit to do good;
In place of cruelty, love rules supreme . . .
And will abolish every evil scheme
Until God's peace for man be understood.

The simple teachings of our Lord are pure,
So that no man may fail to learn and heed . . .
Till righteous peace prevail and hold secure
Against the enemies of human need.
So shall we ever pray, and be one mind,
To bring the way of Truth to all mankind!

Road to Emmaus

The greatest teacher man had ever known
Lay locked and guarded in a silent grave;
And those who knew him well must walk alone . . .
This was their thought – "Himself he could not save."
Two men upon the road felt someone near,
Someone to question them, someone to care,
Whose words of wisdom might relieve their fear –
This friendly stranger would have much to share.

When they reached home, he would have journeyed on
But they implored him to remain awhile . . .
He broke their bread and blest them, and was gone.
The Lord of Life had walked with them each mile!
Out of the tomb he came – alive and free –
To claim his own for all Eternity!

The Great Dream

I "bought" a wondrous dream long years ago,
A dream that lingers, fascinates, and prods;
It was a dream that once was only God's . . .
To keep it, He must let the wide world know.
He dreamed of such a man as would be true,
A righteous man, who'd walk the second mile . . .
Whose love for mankind would be boundless, too,
As boundless as His own – yet hating guile.

To "buy" a dream because the dream was free
And find that it had made the sinner whole,
Increased the value of my human soul
By sudden wealth of immortality.
What wonder that God's dream of Jesus' birth
Meant peace and freedom for the living earth!

And So Today

Today I must do something fine, to make
The way worthwhile, to me alone . . . to me;
And surely I'm not selfish when I take
This attitude – for after all – you see
That's where I live, and there I must begin!
Deep down within this cunning heart of mine
Which plays so many tricks, perhaps some sin
Might lurk . . . therefore I set a light to shine!

Upon this path, where I must walk each day,
Are others like myself, and if I cast
A shadow with my life someone might stray,
Might even lose his way and travel past
The special place he meant to be – and so
Today – I'll try to keep my light aglow!

Child Training

With just a phony toy gun they will stand
By all the brave traditions of a knight . . .
Their sober captain shouts a terse command
And down the line as one, they all face right.
Then swinging tall and straight the little tads
March down the turf quite solemn and sincere,
To meet the enemy like older lads . . .
No wavering, no faltering, no fear.

A sharp swift rat-tat-tat comes from the hedge –
Ambushed again – they fall upon the ground
And worm their flattened bodies to the ledge,
And roll right down the hill without a sound.
One small voice ventures, "Gee, that was a scare.
We shoulda stayed and fought it out up there."

White Trumpets

They brought the lilies — gorgeous, stately, tall —
White trumpets, steady as a golden horn
With high triumphant glory in the call . . .
The Lord was there — for it was Easter Morn.
The people thronging in, their hearts so sure
This day would long survive in memory,
And many hoping it would prove a lure
To bring them often where the soul is free.

Now, from the Chancel, dignified and calm,
The singing choir rose up in sacred praise
Rich toned and vibrant as a joyful Psalm —
While worshipers sit, silently, and gaze.
Like Olden Times — with overflowing grace
They said, "Now surely, God is in this place."

Camp Life

The sky let go with finger streams of bright
To chase the sleeping shadows from their lair;
The call to early watch breaks into flight
As clarion tones wing thru the stilly air.
Each finds a daily silent spot, where youth
Alone, may pause to worship God awhile . . .
And pray for wisdom and the living truth
To guide him over every daytime mile.

The peace of Christian fellowship and grace
Can build a temple out of human clay . . .
And set a light to guard the sacred place
Throughout a camper's life, in one short stay;
From hour to hour as camp life rolls along
A camper's schedule is a merry song!

A Tribute to Johnny

He was a good lad, gentlelike and kind . . .
He left a trail of friendship all the way,
And those who knew him found a peace of mind
With courage to sustain them every day.
The light that touched his cheery path, inspired
His constant effort to pursue the best . . .
And he had never wearied, never tired
Nor lost the grace of God, while on his quest.

While swiftly fading moments gather gain
And grant him time for Scripture and a prayer,
His spirit lifts itself from earthly pain,
And sails away to realms beyond compare.
His faith has etched a shining star in space,
Until we too, shall see the Master's face!

There Is a Way

The world is small, with races not a few . . .
The task is helping each to find its place.
The right to live and flourish in this new
Relationship has brought us face to face
With problems difficult for man to solve.
The trackless wilderness of doubt and fear,
Intolerance and prejudice . . . involve
Mankind today and bring destruction near.

And yet . . . there is a way, so simply planned
A child could follow . . . and the wisest one,
The strongest one on earth, should understand.
It offers peace to every native son . . .
To every pilgrim on a foreign shore . . .
It is the Christian way of life, no more.

To Emilie Dionne

Sweet child of destiny, accept the prize
Excelling priceless jewels in its worth,
Accept the crown of Life not made by earth –
While quiet in the grave thy body lies.
Let thy pure spirit sweep thru gates of might,
And take reward of Him, whose love bestows
That high citation, at the throne of light . . .
Close by the stream where Life eternal flows.

The circle is not broken, but increased . . .
Once visible, defined, and full of song,
Now stretching skyward recently released
It circles Heaven's hallelujah throng.
The warm heart of the world, in spirit glides
To that fair place, where Emilie abides.

Golden Wedding

They are most lovable, they who were wed
A short half-century this current year . . .
And every mile, the golden road has led
Where the hearts are warm and friendships are sincere.
Two charming daughters chose to walk the way
With two strong lads who joined the family pride;
These are the music of their yesterday . . .
Their living Psalm to meet tomorrow's tide.

From green of meadow and the quiet stream
They seek a measure of the Shepherd's grace,
And radiant as the full moon's borrowed gleam
It shines unfailingly upon each face . . .
As if celestial bells intoning night
Had left a benediction, for their light.

Revelation

Dear God, it seems so silly that one man
Could plunge the world into catastrophe . . .
One wild, insane idea, plot and plan
In so short while involve humanity.
Appalling . . . as we try to grasp its might;
Gargantuan beyond the human ken . . .
We only know an evil parasite
Slipped into life and grew and blinded men.

Not quick to judge another country's aim,
As always . . . lovable America
Was basking in the warmth of freedom's flame
When truth flashed straight across our cinema.
Two forces lift a piercing battle cry . . .
And we must help the FREE, or all shall die!

Advent of the Car

My husband's father carried Rural Mail;
The hours were many and the roads quite rough –
And whether heat or dust or frozen trail,
For man and beast, the long day was enough.
When snow lay white and deep upon the ground
His restless worried wife would watch and wait –
And hope for that familiar crunching sound
Of iron clad wheels approaching their front gate.

Then came a day that wheels were rubber shod!
They raced along on roads where mud and rain
Once cut the travel to a patient plod –
They sped him home for lunch – and not in vain.
What luxury – what leisure and good rest –
Awaited faithful carriers – so blest!

To Viola Scott

Our dear Viola from Missouri State
Came into earthly life December One . . .
With silken hair and sleepy eyes she won
The heart of him just eighteen short years late!
You know, that day was Warren's birthday too –
Now he is growing old while you arc young.
But in a far-off city – shining – new –
We'll wait until the golden bell has rung.

So be prepared to come – passport and all,
There'll be no disappointment – no despair,
Just ride off on a cloud, when trumpets call
There's nothing earthly in the golden stair.
The Lord still reigns – the Kingdom still His own,
With Christ the Prince of Peace beside the throne!

Friday

It was a dark day – in reality,
The day our Precious Lord was crucified;
Last night He gave up in Gethsemane,
Submissive and resigned. Today, He died!
Strange darkness hid the sun – the daylight fled
And quiet Earth in wild abandon shook . . .
Till graves, nearby, were emptied of their dead,
And death's strange image could not hide its look!

Now, tenderly kind hands retrieved this form
To place it in a fresh made rock-hewn tomb;
Their hopes are blown away as if by storm,
As loved disciples scatter in the gloom.
So – who can say the day is good – not I –
He cried "It is finished" – and they saw Him die!

At Walnut Manor, San Antonio

They came one morning early — rang my chime.
I called out "Just a minute," and arose . . .
The paperboy collecting, I suppose,
And thought my clock was running short of time.
Then came my big surprise — those lovely gals
All nine, alert and smiling at my door . . .
I had a happy flash — "They are my pals —
My neighbors, living on this very floor."

Upon the card they handed me to read
Were blessings and good birthday wishes too,
And every silent prayer seemed for my need,
For I was facing ninety years — they knew.
We laughed and chatted round the living room
And wondered if a Century Plant might bloom!

Plight

The night comes on, with ease for weary hearts
And sweet surcease for aching flesh and bone;
We sigh a little as the day departs,
And twilight smiles on mortals lying prone.
A certainty — the night was made for rest,
Yet who can calm the fluttering inside
Without a prayer and Christ the Lord as guest
To bless us — that His great love may abide.

Sometimes unfinished tasks distress our sleep
And thoughts in broken dreams begin to flair;
We count the hours, how silently they creep,
Then very soon the day breaks fresh and fair.
"Come unto me," One said, "I'll take your load,
I'll bear your burdens on the toilsome road!"

Temples

Not every Temple is of brick or stone,
Or whitened timber spired amid the trees,
Quiescent, monolithic, and alone . . .
Awaiting Pilgrim songs and humble peas.
Not every altar is enshrined in gems
Of rarest coloring, or golden trim,
Or silver service graved in diadems,
The sacrament immortalizing Him.

But in the glory of a worship day
The spirit of the living God is guest,
While Pilgrims congregate to sing and pray,
And leave reluctantly, as each is blest.
Another Temple, humanly divine . . .
Is every soul's eternal, living shrine!

Sound of Trumpets

He is not dead that left me quite alone,
Companionless and grieved without his love,
He has not vanished in the vast unknown
A twig between his teeth – a long lost dove.
Nor shall he fly thru ageless stars, remote,
For eons in the mystery of space . . .
No, he is answering that high pure note –
That trumpet call, to meet God face to face!

So I shall not presume to be forlorn . . .
The Son of God who died upon the Cross
Became Redeemer – Man became reborn –
And those who worship God are eased of loss.
The presence of a spirit hovers near,
And shall, till sound of trumpets touch my ear!

Toward Jerusalem

They stop along the rugged hillside road
And looking down on proud Jerusalem,
The Lord is torn by prophecies that goad
The soul to weeping, over this fair gem.
Its Temple rises like a sentinel
Above world highways leading to its door,
And thronging quite unlike the years before
The multitudes approach the citadel.

Strange moments tick away to end an age . . .
Alerted angels wait for Calvary;
The Lord's betrayer sets the final stage
To take him captive in Gethsemane.
The sacred supper in the upper room . . .
Old olive trees . . . a garden dark with doom!

Walking Alone

How quietly you left the cherished way
We two had walked. The while you held my hand
I traveled fearlessly . . . Then came the day
I felt your slender fingers loosen . . . and,
You disengaged them, let my hand fall free.
So learned I that to walk alone, one must
Possess a braver heart . . . with alchemy
Of gold, to weather earth's erosive dust.

Brave hearts are polished to a richer gleam
When bared against the elements, to meet
Life's weal. And more I know, that when my feet
Shall touch the waters as I cross the stream,
Familiar fingers . . . warm upon my hand . . .
Will reach to me, from Heaven's borderland!

Miracle

Sun-drenched and silent lay the pregnant fields
Awaiting fullness and the magic tryst —
When bountiful with promise nature yields
Its groaning glory to the ruralist.
Sleek cattle on the far-flung ranges graze
Where equidistant spreads a vast domain . . .
Angoras munch, and sniff the mountain haze,
While ranchmen scan the blue for signs of rain.

The arid day and night cannot avail
To quench the yawning thirst of land and beast —
Only the constant downpour may prevail,
As burning winds presume to sere the feast.
While faithful hearts wait, suddenly, it comes;
It's thunder, like the roll of distant drums!

Escape

A storm looms in the offing as we stroll
The battered windswept beach from east to west:
Wild plunging waters break their frothy roll
And flood the granite boulders where we rest.
Our hope for one short swim seems hope in vain,
A vanguard squall roars down the slender Isle
To sheathe our forms in billowed sand and rain —
Queer manikins, who show the same quaint style.

We amble clumsily from this defeat,
To take a cleansing swim with real delight,
Before a wilder squall proves indiscreet
With undertow to bear us far from sight.
When our brave hearts are homeward bound once more,
The peace of distance dims the stormy shore!

Release

Quite usual a mortal yearns to roam
The verdant hills, or climb steep mountain trails
In search of some deep pool, where nature veils
The peaks in fragrant mists, far, far from home.
He sprawls in rapture on the cool damp sand
To watch a modern liner lift and fly . . .
Reluctantly consigning to the sky
His dreams of flying to a distant land.

He yearns to leave the old familiar way . . .
Adventuring where firebreaks vein the slopes,
Protecting man and tree, and beast of prey . . .
Where dull monotony cannot blast hopes.
The jest is lost in our too small abode . . .
So man sets out upon the open road!

August

Some travel north to find a cooler clime
Where sparkling lakes lie placidly unfurled;
Some go where lofty mountains pantomime
Tall pride, as tho theirs were the only world.
And others travel trainwise to the beach
Where sapphire waves break into snowy crest,
Or fly across the blue Pacific's reach
To rapture where a paradise is blest.

The call of August, clarion and sweet,
Is music to the hearts that love to roam;
But some just keep the watch, with aching feet
That would take flight on journeys far from home.
With one great tree to shelter our abode
We'll wait for springtime and a southern road.

Analogy

I saw the carved-out mountains standing tall
And felt, to paint this, one would surely die . . .
That strength of genius was a gift too small
For such proud beauty piercing God's blue sky.
A shudder grappled like the prick of spines . . .
As curve on curve thru miles of acres rose —
These varied chiseled shapes and strange designs,
To preen their loftiness in stark repose.

Yet, David climbed the hills to ask relief;
Christ sought the mountain solitude for prayer;
Each on a lonely crest poured out his grief
To One who joined them in the silence there.
Sometimes the suddenness of height o'erwhelms
Like answered prayer from Life's eternal realms!

Progress Club

Rare poppies preen their silky loveliness
In pantomime above a crystal bowl,
To let their tall stemmed dignity impress
And etch their beauty on a living scroll.
Bright in their listening, as we, who hear
Sweet music floating thru the rooms to us,
And in a special way our hearts find cheer,
And mellow to the flowing "Angelus."

The spacious home was pantomimed at times,
Performed unknowingly by every guest
To music, story, and the lilt of rhymes . . .
With hospitality its gracious best.
Gay children romp outside to make complete . . .
The freedom of a home where women meet!

Together and Apart

Who robs of individuality
Robs God and robs himself for puny whim . . .
Altho none lives unto himself quite free
Yet each must send his record up to Him.
Each pens his story as it were last page,
With strength to weather shattering events
Lest on the morrow void of good intents,
He may surrender life's true heritage.

None owns, nor can possess another's soul
Whose value is eternal and supreme . . .
The great Creator's realm records the scroll,
Of ownership no mortal can redeem.
In justice man will share another's woe,
Yet each must bear his own, God made it so!

Strenuous Days

And when they knew that Lazarus was dead
They came from Jordan unto Bethany . . .
And Jesus weeping at the graveside said,
"Come forth!" And he came forth, in majesty.
And many watching Jesus now believed
But some sought out the Pharisees and told,
That they may seek him openly, and hold
The Saviour until death had been achieved.

Six days and he must face Jerusalem . . .
The upper room was there, God meant it so;
En route, loved Lazarus would ease the blow
And the annointing would be requiem.
His enemies will draft a subtle plan . . .
That shall rebound with Life for every man!

King of Kings

The King comes riding down a hillside road
And seeing his beloved Jerusalem,
Recalls the story of a strange abode
Where prophecy found life at Bethlehem.
The King had sought to save his native kin
But they rejected him and shunned his face . . .
His great eyes dimmed remembering their sin,
Their desecration of the Holy place.

Amid the fervent spirit of the throng
The Lord Christ rides in quiet dignity . . .
As followers wave branches, and with song
Proclaim him King, to reign triumphantly.
And well he knew that in a few short days
There would be shoutings but no hymn of praise!

Palms and Prophecies

And even as the multitudes acclaim
In loud Hosannas the triumphant King,
The Lord sees only bitter suffering . . .
Jehovah's chosen fallen in their shame.
Once Jesus wept when one he loved had died,
But drops of blood will soon cascade his face,
Yet he sees desolation and disgrace
And Judah's wondrous glory vilified.

There will be stark denial, even thrice,
Ere Peter falls away half-crazed with fear;
But thru the trial, Jesus will appear
Resigned and ready for the sacrifice.
Redemption is approaching highest cost . . .
While the betrayer, gambling high, is lost!

Facing Betrayal

One saw the miracle, and hid inside
The gnawing envy of a jealous heart . . .
For sinful Judas could not quite abide
This gift, while he performed a lowly part.
They seek the more to take Christ by arrest
Since Lazarus came forth, who once was dead . . .
And thus, the wicked one pursued his quest
While following where gentle Jesus led.

The Lord is troubled now; His hour is come.
His dark night of betrayal hovers near . . .
The bargained paltry price, the little sum,
Will buy a potter's field for souvenir.
Sweet spikenard sped the intrigue to white heat,
The deed is done . . . lost Judas strikes defeat!

Facing the Cross

The hour is truly come! Now is the time
To walk the rugged path toward Calvary . . .
The roughest trail the Lord will ever climb,
Yet He was born . . . for such a tragedy.
The supper and the upper room are past . . .
They reach the garden just beyond the brook
Where loved disciples fall asleep at last,
For while He prays, 'tis well they do not look.

There in the garden heavenly seraphim
Give courage and the love of God, for might;
While Judas and the guard lurk in the dim
To hasten Jesus into court, that night.
In vengeance nature screams against the deed,
And Death seems victor, yet, a world is freed!

Facing Resurrection

Long shafts of early light shot thru the gloom,
The morning star seemed lost in wonderment,
As break of day above the silent tomb
Came heralding the glorious event.
The third dawn, dreaded by the enemy,
Adds quake and stormy chaos to their fright,
For God's intrepid angel dazzling white
Rolled back the stone, to set the living free.

The risen Saviour walked once more with men,
His death upon the cross, the open grave,
Are messages to tell and tell again,
To tell the world that Jesus died to save.
Because he rose, we too shall also rise . . .
We, too, shall capture Life's eternal prize!

Glory of the Resurrection

Slowly the dawn's slim fingers animate
The early shadows, usher up the sun
To light the dim horizon, and create
Eternal glory from oblivion.
Then sudden brightness sweeps the silent tomb,
Strikes down the guard and rolls the stone away . . .
Now comes the Saviour from the grave's deep gloom
To meet the promised resurrection day.

The lonely heartbreak of Gethsemane
Sleeps in the garden of remembering . . .
The road that climbed the hill to Calvary
Became immortal when death lost its sting.
Another brighter road climbs higher yet . . .
A freeway up to God, He paid the debt!

Resurrection

The Holy One is vanquished now, it seems,
Their friend is dead . . . His youthful body lies
Within a tomb, and vanquished are their dreams,
Yet He had taught them saying He would rise.
But could He live anew, were they quite sure?
The guilty thought His followers might steal
Their dead, and placed a guard and set a seal,
To make the rock-hewn sepulcher secure.

The eerie gloom hung like a pall at night . . .
The shadows of the third dawn still hung gray,
Then swift angelic glory flashed its light
Struck down the guard and swept the stone away.
The Lord Christ radiantly alive again . . .
Stepped forth, once more, into the world of men!

Remembering His Cross

The slanting shadow of the Cross lies thin
And disappearing, on the barren hill —
Where Golgotha lifts high the world of sin,
As life ebbs out and death clings cold and still.
Untimely darkness covers all the land . . .
Earth shakes, tombs fall apart, the sunlight fails
And sorrow gathers up the little band,
To scatter them on fearful silent trails.

The Cross of Christ is in our midst today
Reminding that between the Ages, gleamed
A lamp of living truth — forever beamed
Upon the excellent, more perfect way.
And those who climb to that eternal place
Shall see the risen Saviour face to face!

Our Nurses

The day is ending – life's bright curtain falls,
Night sleep comes fitfully to weary eyes . . .
Within the sanctity of guarded walls –
Its quiet coverlet the velvet skies.
Along the corridor the silent tread
Of footsteps to gentle someone's pain,
And linger for awhile beside the bed
In reassuring poise – perhaps in vain.

The Angelus is ringing, to intone
The hour, now vacant in its earthly place;
In silence giving up its flesh and bone
To everlasting glory of God's grace.
The moments pass! Another ministry –
Beloved nurses toiling skillfully!

Compassion

One virtue of the many attributes
Ascribed to Christ, is high upon the scale,
Heard often like the clarion of flutes
To rally hope where human strength is frail.
The music of compassion echoing
Along the byways of a broken world . . .
Can banish hate and train the heart to sing
Where once the screaming barbs of vengeance hurled.

Where thin veneer of piety breaks thru
Revealing cruelty and evil trends . . .
The high note of compassion sings anew
To train the marching earth to live as friends.
The end of inhumanity is near
When sweet compassion makes its message clear!

Doors

How sacred is the door to every home
If it be cottage or a stately hall . . .
A penthouse close beneath a starry dome,
A room with but a single outside wall!
Inside is kept a treasure locked and barred,
A tear-stained note, a little toy or shoe,
A photograph all torn and battle scarred;
A sonnet or a book forever new.

And if a heart's door should swing wide and free,
Pray keep forevermore inviolate
The conscious wonder and the mystery
The human crucible may radiate.
And should you find a heart's door cold as steel,
Pray that the love of God might break the seal!

Hopefulness

In early wilderness men gave humble thanks
For home and shelter in a land their own . . .
For freedom flowing in their hearts' full banks
And for the earth's good yield their hands had sown,
For tangled vastness yet to be explored.
A brave new faith sprang up in every man
That mystery of ages wrought and stored
Might greet their long awaited caravan.

They met each flaming dawn courageously
Partaking richly of God's love and grace,
Extolling Him in simple dignity
For beauty of the sky and earth's broad space.
That same high spirit of the yesteryear
Shall some day free the world of doubt and fear!

Orchids to the Valiant

Come, look with me across the tragic scenes
That stain the pages of the century . . .
That press in stark relief against the greens
Where flowers grew, and children romped with glee.
Look for the beauty and magnificence . . .
Behold the carnage dripping red with blood
Where tall lads fought in reeking stench and mud
To block the force of demon violence.

Now they have come again, that blighting horde,
To strip the earth of faith and brotherhood . . .
To break our wills. They've taken up the "sword"
To flay and blast, to conquer all the good.
With what stupidity does Satan ply . . .
For Truth and Righteousness shall never die!

To Billy Pilgreen

The lad was four – this keen eyed little boy
Who cantered off to make a morning call;
The early day meant naught to him at all,
So with a merry heart he pranced for joy.
The sky was dull and he took note of it
And pondered the mysterious delay . . .
Could be . . . God holding back the sun, a bit;
Then scampered off to have a morning play.

He thought the neighbor's house was very still
And to his great surprise found her abed . . .
"Not on the job" were mighty thoughts for Bill;
Quite mystified, he sauntered home and said
(As nonchalantly as a learned one) . . .
That even ". . . God had not put up the sun."

Futurity

Now, since it seems befitting to proclaim
That man, upon surviving certain years,
Disqualifies . . . let us concede; the same
Cannot apply to each, lest there be fears.
If men walk down the path where shadows fall
And time presents that dread futurity
By sounding of a tragic trumpet call . . .
How now, shall age compete with penury?

Now, in this wondrous land we should be kin;
As touching vital things learn tolerance . . .
That neither youth nor aged know chagrin;
That brotherhood may have predominance.
Look now! As true Americans, behold! . . .
This land is FREE, alike, for young and old!

Dimes for Dear Ones

She was so lovely with her golden hair
And laughing eyes. And fleet as any deer!
He was so beautiful, so strong, so fair . . .
And they had never known the sting of fear.
Then, still as night a slinking monster crept,
With blow as sudden as a pointed blade,
To strike their lithe young bodies as they slept;
And when 'twas done, two cripples had been made.

Today, pain-twisted bodies lie and wait,
And young minds wonder when the day will come
To let them walk again, and run, and skate . . .
But you will never find their spirits glum,
For they are counting on a nation's dimes
To give them health again, and happy times!

A New World

Remote from devastation's bitter woe,
Some have a feeling of security . . .
Protected by a force that seems to flow
With ease and comfort in a land so free.
But if transported to a distant isle
Where shock and horror of a crashing raid
Reveal the power of a loathsome guile . . .
We'd hasten our defense, and send them aid.

Our hearts ache at the very thought of it,
But not a patriot who would not die
To save America . . . nor one submit
To laws which we do not exemplify.
And from Democracy's travail, the shorn
And tortured world shall one day be reborn!

Birth of Freedom

What cataclysmic eras have combined
To cast their spell upon bewildered man!
With furrowed brow, and facial contour lined,
He scans the infamous barbarian.
He looks beyond the present savage horde
To dynasties and governments of old . . .
Where ancient pagan rulers, sated, bored,
Feast greedy eyes upon another's gold.

He looked again, and from the blood and smoke
Arose a rallying triumphant cry . . .
And when the stunned embattled world awoke,
The Flag of Freedom floated in the sky!
And from that mast, above the tyrant's frown,
No foe on earth shall ever drag it down.

Beautiful Free America

Some dark forboding shadows still remain
Which could recede and quietly disappear
If hearts gave thanks to God for this terrain,
For fearless pioneers who settled here.
Brave creatures from the nations of the Earth
Faced hardships quite unknown across the sea;
They built a nation in the wilds of dearth,
Fought man and beast – and soil – to keep it free.

Our days are stormy – mighty billows roll
But we shall trust the providential hand
To guide our sailing, by the high bright goal –
Upstanding – tall and safe upon our land.
America – Beloved of all the World,
Still young, your banners fly the wind, unfurled!

Gethsemane

There in the shadows of Gethsemane
The bitter brimming cup was at His lip,
While all alone in deepest agony
Great drops of bloody sweat begin to drip.
At such a time as this His dearest friends
Lay fast asleep from overweariness –
Not even dreaming how the battle ends;
But Angels came to ease His great distress.

"Not my will but my Father's will be done";
And finding them still sleeping, said "Sleep on,
Now – take your rest"; the battle had been won
The agony, the fight he waged, were gone!
Our agonies and battles too shall fade
When we consign our wills – the price is paid!

Sacred Journey

Sacred Journey

I'd like to walk along some silent trail
Where Jesus' feet stepped lightly down its length,
That I might feel the salty sea-blown gale
And stand long in a boat — to know His strength.
I'd like to wander where the mountainside
Once chambered in its cleft His wondrous voice,
Where principle and precept stemmed the tide
Till doubt let go, and truth compelled a choice.

I'd like to touch the dust upon the place
Where Peter's words, "Thou art the Christ," rang true,
And capture if I may some bit of grace
Left hidden for a traveler's residue.
And there on Olivet, I'm sure I'd find,
The mantle of His spirit left behind!

The Journey

As pilgrims jog along toward Bethlehem
To pay the tax at their ancestral place . . .
The journey seems a solemn requiem
To days when Judah lived within God's grace.
They chanted Psalms and things the prophets told,
Of wealth and glory lost to wicked hands,
Of Temple vessels wrought of precious gold
Purloined by enemy marauding bands.

Thru hours of idle plodding on the trail . . .
The mingled song and thoughts of sacred lore
Eased weary hearts as if a heavenly veil
Hid troublous visions at their daily door.
This must be grooming for that wondrous night,
So soon to startle shepherds with its light!

Reclaiming His Own

He walked the miles to reach blue Galilee,
In search of those he loved, and missed of late;
And there they were, upon a fishless sea —
Sleep-weary, toiling thru the night, they wait.
The restless boat, the empty net, at dawn,
Are grim reminders . . . for each empty heart.
There was no living now, no going on,
No one to bid their anxious fears depart.

A voice calls . . . "Cast the net on the other side."
"The Lord," one shouts, "and he has words for us";
Soon men and boat and fishes ride the tide
To One who made their toil victorious.
He cooked some fish to eat, and they could tell
He loved them, needed them, and all was well!

Forevermore Immortal

The early hour is pointing toward the dawn
Only the morning star shows thru the gloom . . .
Night's drapery, still hanging closely drawn,
Enshrouds the Saviour in the silent tomb.
So sure of victory, the sting of death
Leans heavily against the Holy One . . .
If time could deviate immortal breath
The Lord would fall into oblivion.

But Heaven sends its power in dazzling might
Strikes down the guard and rolls the stone away;
The grave is flooded with a brilliant light
And Christ steps into Resurrection Day!
Immortal Life has won — the sting is gone,
The Kingdom of the living God moves on!

From Life to Life

I walk along a busy city street
Where teeming thousands press their eager way,
Intent upon a destination . . . fleet
Of foot, impatient at each slight delay.
Where are they going in such a haste? They seem
The self-same people on parade, the whole
Of day . . . some sad, some worn; some faces beam.
What are their thoughts; and what, their distant goal?

I watch the hourglass hanging on my wall
As telltale sands of time flow swiftly thru
Its narrow pass . . . and suddenly recall
The hurried throng. Like sands of time we, too,
Negotiate a gaged receptacle . . .
As, Life to Life, transcribes the miracle.

Blessing and Honor

Along the distance since Neanderthal
The varied Ages should evaluate
This Age — Supreme — a piercing trumpet call
Announcing breakthru to uncharted fate.
This fabulous achievement of mankind
Came screaming from a caverned trilogy —
Man's inner depth of soul and heart and mind
Primed by the source of creativity.

We pray that patterns, progress may release,
Will merit acclamation and applause . . .
And give to all the world a righteous peace
Ennobling man and honoring God's laws.
Inherent genius lights a taller flame . . .
To laud creation's Master with its fame.

Lady of the Manse

Few know the heart of her who chose a way
Requiring courage and ability . . .
And sharing others' griefs, to live each day
As tho the living patterned easily.
To wear a gracious manner and sincere,
No matter what the anguished hours contain . . .
To be content with those who are quite near,
And be a friend to all in her domain!

Along this path she would keep pace with him,
Share countless happy problems, all his woe;
Be teacher, leader, counselor . . . must know
How precious are the frivolous, the grim.
Ah, yes, and more . . . quite unperturbed she sighs,
God's own would never have it otherwise!

Storms

Above the night winds raging steadily,
The cry of bird and beast in mingled fear
Comes weird and fierce in plaintive savagery . . .
A warning to their kind that death rides near.
Bent down and bowing low, and lower still,
The palm and oleander moan and weep . . .
Sharp flashes strike, and trees protest in shrill
Bewildered wailings, as the stab cuts deep.

Man prays and trembles, hoping his abode
Will ride the storm at anchor and endure,
While bitter lashings crash and sway, and goad
The mortal into momentary cure.
Then God's proud creatures, proudest of them, men
In humble pride lift up their world . . . again!

To Lela Riley

Our hearts are tender, in the radiant cheer
That brightens all the weary world, again . . .
And in the quiet of this hour, we hear
The echo of that first "goodwill toward men."
We see the frightened shepherds, as they rush
Across the fields, and down the rugged road
Where Glory hugs a little town, to hush
Its clamoring beside a quaint abode.

As we behold, upon your countenance,
And in your life . . . that same reflected gleam,
Our hearts grow warmer in that radiance,
As faith and hope and love . . . reflect your dream.
We lift the latch, our heart's door stands ajar,
Abide with us . . . and share the Eastern Star!

Golden Wedding Trip

Seems only yesterday that we were wed
Yet fifty precious years have come and gone . . .
The days, the months, the years have quickly fled
And we keep teaching, preaching, on and on.
Missouri was our state, but came a time
We entered school together far from home;
And we still count the ministry sublime,
Still love God's work wherever we may roam.

Now as this quite momentous date of all
Approaches in September . . . we shall go
Just for the going, in the early fall,
Out where the blue Pacific waters flow.
As wild terrain and golden valleys vie
We'll ride the long streamliner whizzing by!

To Billy Woodward

Words are so futile, yet possess a great strength,
Can lift a nation or destroy a world . . .
The sacred Word gives life, and at its length
A scroll of Life Eternal is unfurled.
Words can enslave a starving populace
Or ease their hunger with a magic food,
Immersing mind and body in God's grace . . .
Till sin and death retreat and wars conclude.

Sometimes in meditation, words reveal
Such beauty, in portrayal and design,
They stir the heart, and liberate the real,
Transforming life to something true and fine.
So, let the silence of his speech portray,
In excellence, that bright Immortal Way!

The Gate Shall Not Prevail

This is the tragic day of white-hot hate
Fronting the wrath against the tyrant's lie,
When flaming crossbeams rise to crucify . . .
And FREEDOM struggles to perpetuate.
The righteous anger of the Just is late . . .
The swinging pendulum, now low, now high,
Shall swing till destiny . . . But live or die,
The Just have stormed perdition's mighty gate.

They are so young, that saved Democracy . . .
So brave, so strong, so wholly confident;
So trained and poised they battled righteously.
Their broken bodies form the Testament
All men will read . . . until Eternity,
And reading shall grow wise . . . and reverent!

Spirit of Cavell

Today . . . her memory reminds of days
That will not fade. The intervening years
Have brought no surcease from the dismal haze
That blots out reason, chills the heart with fears;
Frustration floods the calm exterior! . . .
Blue lights! Blackouts! The surge of marching feet!
What is this force that renders men inferior . . .
When there is much, to make a man complete?

The footprints of Cavell, so firmly pressed
Upon humanity's broad thoroughfare . . .
Lead upward to a shrine! Upon our quest
Could we but feel her tranquil spirit there,
Our spirits, answering, would find release . . .
And all earth's nations would consent to peace.

Brother . . . Father . . . Husband

To Georgia Edgeworth

Our precious thoughts are strewn along the trail
Like flowers, leaving in the atmosphere
A fragrance, that survives the wildest gale . . .
Preserving memories alive and clear.
Our years are in the passing . . . this we know;
There shall be heartbreak tears, and sad good-byes,
But souls will never lose that shining glow
Reflected from the bright of Heaven's skies.

O soul . . . thou rarest gift of God to man;
When you shall step across the great divide
To enter realms where death cannot reside,
The Lord Himself will glorify the span.
For you have reached supernal ecstasy . . .
That wondrous goal . . . your Immortality!

To Roy Brown

He was so young to travel on a strand
No one on Earth today had walked along . . .
His years were spread across a greening land
Where joy of toil gave life its rhythmic song.
His home and family, close friends and God
Contrived a pleasant pattern for his days . . .
Gave hope and healing to his gentle ways,
And courage on the rugged miles he trod.

But this was one short pathway set aglow:
A choir of trumpets playing high and clear,
The sound of welcome only Angels know . . .
God's glory reaching out to draw him near.
Not by imagination's highest flight . . .
Can man portray that realm, which has no night!

Similarity

Tall trees reach up to touch the lofty dome
But know too well, that aim cannot be won . . .
Yet in their sapling days small roots find home
With anchorage for climbing toward mid-sun.
All thru the years, a century or more,
That same projecting force inched up their crown,
Unyielding and determined as of yore . . .
As though God saw the struggle and looked down.

There is perfection on that high bright range
Which beckons, beckons, night and day and year,
While mortals marvel at the magic change
As miracle of seasons perseveres.
Man, too, may labor for perfection's goal
And grow a finer fabric for his soul!

To Dr. Paul L. Barone

I saw a great man on his daily quest
And read his thoughts in olden skills and new . . .
His step was quiet and his words were few
While probing for the ultimate and best.
Ofttimes his smile would light another's face,
His kindly touch smooth out a furrowed brow . . .
And troubled hearts would cease to ache, somehow,
Secure and trusting in his skill and grace.

And there was dedication for each day;
Research and lofty aims for honest pride,
And always wisdom prompted him to pray
That God's creative vision be his guide.
Most evident . . . the faith to persevere
Inscribed his handiwork year after year!

Warren
In the Chapel

The spirit vanished quietly and free,
Without the earthly garment of his years –
Now lying in serene sublimity,
Bereft and lone before our flowing tears.
The pendulum swings hour by hour in rhyme,
As tho to sympathize – keep faith with us
Throughout this holy interim of time,
Which seems so tragic and mysterious.

We watch and mourn because our love is true,
Because the glory of our service here,
Will keep fond memories forever new
And give our lonely hearts their needful cheer.
Our faith shall live as long as we survive,
And open Heaven's gate, when we arrive.

Fading to Bloom Again

I do not wonder, as the days fade out
And take the elderly along with them,
That some stay on until there is no doubt
That God created New Jerusalem.
I do not grieve, as days pass into years
And eyes grow dimmer in the sunlit air . . .
I know — as life is fading, drenched with tears,
That God will dry them in the Great Somewhere.

And always near me are encircling arms
To hold my broken earthly life awhile —
So I thank God and harbor no alarms
That every step leads into that last mile.
But O, how thrilling as I look behind —
Reluctant still — to leave God's humankind.

Dawning of Eternity

O, may I still be kind if kindness fails
When all of good seems to preclude its worth —
And loving care heals not when pain assails
To ravish these few precious days on earth.
Courageous values lost their sense of sight
As pain's long vigil gnaws at flesh and bone . . .
And truly we shall reach our darkest night
Should deep calamity become our own.

When sound of Life's loved clarion, once clear,
Once free and vibrant, on the morning air —
Seems almost vanished in the atmosphere,
It's time for Angelus to ring for prayer.
O dawn, how steadily thy brilliance beams —
God's champion, beyond man's fondest dreams.

The Lord Christ Jesus

He traveled on a road — a dusty road . . .
His life became a barter and a scorn;
When hungry, sought a field and ate some corn,
For there was no place called the Lord's abode.
He knew the River Jordan, knew it well
And never ceased to feel its cleansing touch
Nor fail to rank its value as of such
That left a story for the world to tell.

His few short years slipped cautiously away . . .
Forgetting all the tragic agony
He speaks his last undying words one day,
Then being lifted up — rose silently —
While those he loved sped toward Jerusalem,
For power to teach the whole wide world, thru them!

Unconquerable Democracy

What is this force that takes such deadly toll,
That sets its mark with calculating aim
To drive its fang into a nation's soul?
The wound gapes lifeless! Dry! What is its name?
Is there no surcease from such venom? Must
The strife continue until death shall end
What once was Freedom and Democracy? Dust
To dust! What mockery! What bitter blend!

But even as this arid well yawns deep
Within the heart of man, another spring
Blows forth to send its purifying leap
In torrents, to baptize the world . . . to bring
Again the miracle of healing grace
To all the nations . . . and to every race!

Claudia

O Claudia, from starlit realms above,
The soft sweet sound of music in your name
Comes drifting down, reminding of your love –
And always, evermore, shall be the same.
The one bright melody that lives in us –
To still the sudden rush of earthly tears,
To lift the heart beyond the silent years,
That life anew may be victorious!

Dear Claudia, how can I tell of ways
So motherly, so loving, that her kin
Revere and honor her with highest praise
And cling to her for fondest discipline.
The world o'erflows with mothers – saints they are –
But find a Claudia, will take you far!

America Today

The whole world waited long for this great land –
So rugged, so adaptable and so lush . . .
Awaited people brave and lone, who stand
For righteousness, while deep in underbrush.
It took a miracle to pull them thru
The multiplicity of life's affairs,
Where every wrested mile – they must subdue
The wild, untamed, which leaped up unawares.

Those who were truly fortunate survived;
The young, the sickly could not win, deprived
Of human strength; themselves they could not save,
And many perished who were strong and brave.
The miracle of progress was the flame,
That burned the dross, that brought this country fame!

To Be American

Their poverty was clean! They sang a lot –
Sang songs of their beloved Southland home;
Tho fields spread out for miles and days were hot
They never thought of leaving them to roam.
The soil was sacred far above its worth –
Where, in the balmy twilight mammies hum
As children doze and lazy banjos strum –
Close by the very cabin of their birth.

Yet this could not suffice for love of lore . . .
A change had come with learning – like a flame,
To gain that knowledge held in greater store,
They spread their wings and flew in steady aim.
Then, on the stormy lanes, as others found –
They settle for their place on holy ground!

My Country 'Tis of Thee

They were not hicks, those men who loved and farmed
The bright fresh soil awaiting their kind hand.
For centuries the rich loam lay unharmed –
For only moccasins had trod the land.
The inborn genius of the farmer's skill –
Determination, and abiding grace,
Had matched his innate wish to still
The rising turmoil of this peaceful place.

In early years their very lives were lost
In mounting troubles as they worked their farms,
Then people – good and bad – at any cost –
Began to build and live above alarms.
They learned to listen to the still small voice
Reminding – God had one day made a choice.

The Space Age

Is there no way to humanize this Age?
It should have purified mankind on sight!
But there were few to write upon the page —
And few who could explain the outer flight.
It was explosive to the human thought,
And quite too much for man to comprehend
So — feeling almost obsolete — distraught —
It seemed the common man had reached the end.

That higher thinking mortals might incline
To supercede or disregard the plan
So long familiar, in the World design.
Then — I looked up to God — He loves the man!
And I am too unlearned to predicate —
To offer one small word to change his fate!

Restoration

The quiet glory of a climbing hill
Finds climax where the sky and treetops meet . . .
Where stillness permeates my flagging will,
Dispelling every shadow of defeat.
Within the dusky solitude of trees
Their gentle breathing cools the noonday shade . . .
Drips moisture on the fragrant gypsy breeze
To fluff my spiney bed, the years have made.

At twilight starry lanterns seem to string
Their twinkling shapes on branches near the earth,
While hidden in the glimmer, night birds sing
To stately pines of their intrinsic worth.
Soon dawn's kind hands bring to my resting place
The spotless mantle of redeeming grace!

Silence

There is the silence of an aching heart,
Too deeply silent for a tear or moan;
And there's a silence after friends depart,
When for a time, life dips to monotone.
There's breathless silence that precedes a storm,
Which grass and leaves, and creeping things all know;
Ecstatic silence . . . as a girlish form
Kneels at the altar, in a dream tableau.

That awful silence of a captured land . . .
Wrapped in the cloak of muted slavery,
When count of time is lost; sans liberty;
Hating, praying, but daring not to stand.
God, in the silence make our thought sublime,
That we may think aright . . . in aftertime!

Peace on Earth

O Peace, thou wanderer upon the Land
In search of those to love you all their days,
Can you not find them walking hand in hand
Across the crowded Earth on peaceful ways!
Go plant the golden seeds and plant them well
Where blooms will open windows toward the sky,
Then watch the wonder of the magic spell
To capture hearts as they go passing by.

Peace, Peace, how great the task, and workers few,
But one truth planted in the heart of man
Can yield a shining harvest – sacred – new,
To implement God's holy peaceful plan!
How beautiful are they at reaping time –
Who bring God's peace to every precious clime.

Learning to Fly

This parting night brought quietness to each;
The silver moon, the stars, the southern breeze
Blown softly from the Gulf . . . no need of speech,
With fingers twined, eyes tender, to appease.
All this was proof they'd woven far too late
Their tapestry of silent lingering,
And suddenly they knew that dreams must wait,
For suddenly . . . they were remembering!

Tomorrow she will stare in wonderment,
As high above the fleecy clouds his plane
Takes flight for some far distant field, to train.
Just now, they sense a sudden sentiment
Too close to tears . . . a kiss and then good-bye;
For love, for home, for Country . . . he must fly!

Tribute:
George Washington

Born in the truly green years of our Land . . .
With vigilance that swept the vast domain
And took the strength of genius to maintain,
He grew to manhood knowing where to stand.
To broad expanse of nature's grass and trees,
To distances between the little towns
Where rugged lanes were not traversed with ease
He gave no heed, nor lined his brow with frowns.

From innate wisdom came his learning skill,
And excellence of manner as a youth . . .
From choice associations and good will
Gained keen appreciation of the Truth
So — loving life — down to his last faint breath,
He served his cherished country until death!

In Memoriam
Rev. R. Warren Main
1879-1973

Ship a-Sailing

The Angelus
    Is ringing now –
Across the prow
    I see white caps
Atop the swell –
    The water laps
But all is well,
    Is well
At Evening bell,
    Evening bell.

The Angelus
    Is ringing softly
Now!
    The Angelus
At Evening bell
    And all is well,
Is well . . . is well!